HARISH DAMODARAN

INTRODUCING

ADVAITA

Contents

Preface

Advaita Vedanta is one of the most influential Schools of Philosophy in India. It reached its zenith of glory with its main proponent Jagat Guru Adi Sri Sankaracharya, a sage who lived for just 32 years but worked miracles like commenting on important texts of Vedanta, conducting arguments with scholars, and traveling all over India establishing the unity of the Nation.

Advaita Vedanta has thousands of books written on its various topics. However, there are not many that may be of some help to the beginners who are interested in Indian Philosophy, religion and culture. The author of this book himself had to struggle a lot because of this during his studies. This is an attempt to serve the purpose of a new comer, though the author does not claim any authority.

The work would not have been possible without the kind support and encouragement of Dr. T.S. Girishkumar, Mahatma Gandhi University, Kerala, India.

Chapter 1

Advaita: The Evolution of the School

The four Vedas- Rig Veda, Yajur Veda, Sama Veda and Atharva Veda- contain the oldest record of philosophical thinking in the world. Besides Vedas and Upanisads, each system of Indian Philosophy, which is designated as darsana, has its own source books such as sutras, Bhashyas etc. Sutras contain highly condensed form of philosophic thought and hence require interpretations and commentaries for ordinary men to follow their meaning. Examples of Sutras are: Nyaya Sutra of Gautama, Samkhya Sutra of Kapila, Yoga sutra of Patanjali, Vedanta Sutra of Badarayana etc.

A commentary on the Sutra is called Bhashya. For example Sutra Bhashya of Sankaracharya, Sri Bhashya of Sri Ramanuja-both are commentaries on Vedanta Sutra of Badarayana.

Six orthodox Indian Schools of thought or Sad darsanas namely - Nyaya of Gautma, Vaisesika of Kanada, Samkhya of Kapila, Yoga of Patanjaly, Mimamsa of Jaimini and Vedanta of Badarayana - accept the authority of the Vedas: Yet, the Nyaya, Vaisesika, Samkhya and Yoga do not originate from vedas; but from corresponding sutras. Mimamsa and Vedanta, unlike the other four thoughts of the Orthodox group are direct interpretations of Vedic Philosophy. Jaimini in his Mimamsa Sutra, interprets Karmakanda (Mantras, Brahmanas and Aranyakas) portion of Vedas, as giving the real purport of Vedas; where as, Vedanta Sutra is upholding Jnanakanda portion (Upanisads) as of philosophic worth. The two sutras; Mimamsa and Vedanta, together investigate the whole of vedic philosophy.

The term 'Vedanta' literally means the end of the vedas , which are the Upanisads. The views of Upanisads also constitute the final aim of the Vedas or the essence of the Vedas. The Vedanta sutra of Badarayana, the classical Upanisads such as Isa, Kena, Katha , Prasna, Mundaka, Mandukya, Aitareya, Taittiriya, Chandogya and Brihadaranyaka together with Bhagavad gita constitute the fundamental texts of Vedanta school. These three sources -Upanisads , the Vedanta Sutra and Bhagavad Gita- belong to three different catagories or prastanas. The Upanisads belong to Sruti prasthana, Vedanta Sutra to Nyaya Prasthana, and and the Bhagavad Gita to Smriti Prasthana. Hence these three texts are together called prasthana thraya (three prasthanas) of the Vedanta darsana.

The Vedanta Sutra is also known as Brahma Sutra because it is an exposition of the doctrine of the Brahman. This is again called Saririka Sutra because it deals with the embodiment of the unconditional self. Thus unlike the

Mimamsa Sutra of Jaimini that investigates the duties enjoined by the veda, together with rewards there to, the vedanta Sutra of Badarayana describes the philosophical and theological views of the Upanisads. It is a systematic investigation of the various views of the Upanisads.

The Vedanta Sutra consists of 550 Sutras. The sutras are highly intelligible by themselves and leave everything to the interpreter.

As a result, we get different kinds of Vedantic schools, of which Sankaracarya's Advaita, Sri Ramanuja's VisistAdvaita and Madhvacarya's Dvaita are most famous. These three Schools are noteworthy because they represent three distinct ways of understanding the ultimate reality, the Brahman. Advaita stresses the non-dualistic view, VisistAdvaita stands for the qualified non-dualistic view and dvaita puts forward the dualistic view, and all these schools base their different arguments on Brahma Sutra by giving different interpretations.

The Vedanta Sutra has four adhyayas (chapters)-Samanvaya, Avirodha, Sadhana and Phala. The first namely Samanvaya adhyaya deals with theory of Brahaman. Its purpose is reconciliation of the different views on the Brahman such as cosmic view, acosmic view etc.

The second chapter is called Avirodha adhyaya where the author meets the objections brought against these views of Brahaman and he criticizes the rival theories.

The third chapter is called Sadhana adhyaya in which the ways and means of attaining Brahama Vidya is discussed in detail.

The fourth and last chapter namely Phala adhyaya deals with the fruits of Brahama Vidya, and also the description of pitryana (rituals to ancestors) and devayana (way to devotion).

For Badarayana, Veda is eternal. He declares that there is no possibility of discovering metaphysical truth by means of tarka (yukthy) or reflection. Sruti and Smriti are two sources of knowledge. By Sruti Badaryana meant Upanidas and by Smriti he meant Bhagavad geeta, Mahabharata, and code of Manu (Manusmriti). Smriti is dependent on sruti. But Sruti is independent and self-evident. But, to the question whether cosmic view or acosmic view is the higher view, Sutra does not give a clear answer. There fore, Adi Sankaracharya interprets the Sutra view as acosmic view, while, both Sri Ramanuja and Madhavacharya interpret the same as cosmic view. It is on the acosmic view, thus, the doctrine of Advaita is built upon.

By interpreting the Brahma Sutra in the acosmic way, the Advaitin gains a logical footing upon which they can keep their school of thought, Advaita in perfect balance.

Sruti is the name given to the Vedas and the Upanisads which are treated with great respect in Advaita philosophy. The term 'Sruti' means that which is heard. Sages, by long disciplines and preparations, made them fit vehicles for receiving and conveying the eternal truth to the rest of the mankind. Sruti gives us what has occurred in the intuitive minds of the saints and the sages at the time of exalted imagination. Hence, Sruti is the word of the Absolute.

In Advaita view the Upanishads are for the sake of the establishment of the immediate experience of Brahman. They are capable of generating immediate as well as mediate knowledge. For example the statement “you are the tenth man” certainly results immediate knowledge of one man being the tenth person for the one who lost himself in counting. Like wise, by listening to the Upanisads one can get immediate intuition of Brahman. If one does not experience so, it is not because the Upanisads are incapable of it. It is only because there is no reasoning involved.

According to Advaita, the Brahman alone is real and it is known by Sruti. But Sruti itself is unreal in the third and highest level of reality. Though unreal, it can sublate the illusory world and reveal Brahman. It is like roar of the dream-lion that can wake one up.

The Scriptures (the Vedas and the Upanisads) are the record of spiritual experience and they do convey an idea of what the Ultimate is like. The special merit of the Scriptures lie in that they alone can reveal any knowledge about the Ultimate.

The Scriptures are composed of sentences or vakyas which in their turn, are composed of words arranged in specific order so as to convey certain meaning words are the vehicles of thought. ‘Sabda’ means sound and word. Sabda pramana is, thus the knowledge derived from the authority of words.

The Advaitins have commentaries on all the ten important upanisads and one later Upanishad. They are Isa, Kena, Katha, Prasna, Mandukya, Chandogya, Thaithiriya, Aithareya, Mundaka and Brihadaranyaka along with Svetasvaratha.

The Advaita interprets the Upanisads as the proclamations of acosmic view of the Brahman. Whatever appears to be describing the cosmic view of the Brahman is ascribed to the vyavaharika level of reality. It is meant for the ordinary people to understand the basic principles of philosophy. So, it must not be taken up as anti-Advaitic. All descriptions of whole and parts absolute and relative, finite and infinite are transcendent in the Brahman.

When the Isavasya Upanishad declares "isavasyam idam sarvam", the Advaitin interprets it in an un-orthodox way. Traditional meaning is that "the Lord Isvara dwells everywhere in this world." But the Advaitin explains this as "the world must be covered with Isvara" and so on and this does not harm the Advaitic concept of "Jagat midhya".

The Mundaka Upanishad Speaks pure Advaita when it describes the individual soul, like an arrow reaches the target the Brahman and becomes one with it.

In this way, all the major Upanisads are skill fully interpreted in the Advaitic line of thinking. Thus, we can see that the Sruti never contradicts the doctrines of the Advaita Vedanta. Sruti, in fact, has given the philosophical back ground upon which the system of Advaita stands.

The Bhagavad Gita (the song celestial) belongs to the Smriti Prasthana. It is an important source of the school of Advaita. Of the three prasthanas, the upanisads (Sruti prasthana) give the philosophical back ground for Advaita, where as, the Brahma Sutra (Nyaya prasthana) supplies a logical standpoint of reason. The Advaitins look forward to the third prasthana, the Bhagavad Gita, for the guidelines to practice Advaita in daily life. According to them the Bhagavad Gita teaches how to live a life worthy of living, in accordance with the system of Advaita.

The Bhagavad Gita is the teaching of Lord Sri Krishna to Arjuna on the battle field of Kurukshetra. The Bhagavad Gita's importance in the religio-philosophical literature of India is second only to the Upanisads. The poem, with its 18 chapters form a part of the great epic Mahabharata, where it describes the two rival armies of the Pandavas and the Kauravas engaged against each other.

The occasion, which calls forth the teaching is of extreme seriousness (when the fate of the country as well as the righteousness in peril). It is written in a simple and charming style and is in the form of a dialogue, which gives it a dramatic appearance. The massage that it gives is of supreme value and is applicable to every man in every country. It does not discuss in detail any deep philosophical problems or subtle details of ethics; but only gives broad principles relating to term. The most significant attraction of the Bhagavad Gita is its spirit of tolerance, which is the most important characteristic of Indian thought.

The central teaching of the Bhagavad Gita is actionism or karma yoga. To understand clearly the meaning of 'Karma yoga', the words 'Karma' and 'Yoga' are to be analyzed separately. 'Karma' means 'what is done' or 'a deed'. Karma Signifies that particular form of activity, which is taught in the Karma Kanda of the Vedas namely sacrifice (yoga). But in Bhagavad Gita it signifies duty in accordance with custom and tradition, which were found, associated at the time with particular section or class of people, the Varnadharmas, as they are called. Again Karma is used in a sense as to signify divine worship or devotional duty (puja).

The meaning the Bhagavad Gita admits for Karma is that of 'Social obligation'. The word 'yoga' means 'harnessing' or 'applying to oneself. So by 'karma yoga' the Bhagavad Gita means 'devotion to the discharge of social obligation'.

The Bhagavad Gita stresses 'nishkama karma' or performing the duties without the least desire for its results. People do karmas because they are attracted by the fruits of the karmas (Karma phala). This is not the kind of the karma, the Bhagavad Gita advocates because this kind of Karma is not pure. It is tainted by desire (Kama). For the 'song celestial', Karma is not a means to an end, but an end in itself. There fore, the aim of the result must be dismissed all together from the mind, before as well as during the act. Such an act is called 'nishkama karma' or selfless action.

The Advaitins have not even the slightest objection to the concept of the nishkama karma. They accept it whole-heartedly. This forms the pragmatic side of the Advaita Vedanta.

Again for those who cannot take up 'Karma yoga', the Bhagavad Gita suggests 'Karma Sanyasa'. That is, through renunciation too, the seeker can find his liberation. This, also, is in tune with the Advaitic View. One who is in the Paramarthika level of reality is above and beyond all the Karmas.

The Bhagavad Gita puts forward, the concept of the Sthitha prajna. The Sthitha prajna is a man of steady wisdom. He is liberated from the chain of endless karmas. He is the Jivan Mukta upon whom Advaita Vedanta showers all its praises.

The picture of the God, Purushotama, as shown by the Bhagavad Gita suits to the Suguna Brahman or Isvara of the Advaita Vedanta. He is the very embodiment of existence, essence and excellence of all the qualities.

Thus, in short the Bhagavad Gita, as a source book, saves the philosophy of Advaita Vedanta from the danger of being other-worldly and self- centered.

This divine song shows the light to follow the right path for the Advaitins. It tells them how to live and how to act. It is the real path to liberation.

Among the secondary sources of the Advaita Vedanta, the Mandukya Karika by Sri Gaudapada Acharya holds a very high position. Gaudapada Acharya is the Guru of the Guru of Sri Sankaracharya and therefore, known as the 'Parama Guru'.

On the first look, the Mandukya Karika is a commentary on the Mandukya Upanishad. But, in fact, by writing a commentary on the Mandukya Upanishad, Sri Gaudapada Acharya is establishing the system of Advaita Vedanta.

Sri Gaudapada Acharya bases his philosophy on the doctrine of no-origination or 'ajathi vada'. Through the Mandukya Karika (other wise called Gaudapada Karika), he establishes the reality of non-dual self.

The Mandukya Upanishad begins with the equation Aum = Brahman = Self and proceeds to describe the three states of the self viz; Jagrat (waking), Swapna (Dreaming), Sushupti (deep sleep) and Thuriya (Forth stage). Sri Gaudapada Acharya makes this declaration of the Upanishad as the basis of his metaphysical quest and seeks to show through reasoning that no originate is the final truth.

The Gaudapada Karika gives clear evidence that Sri Gaudapada Acharya is the first systematic exponent of Advaita Vedanta. The central principles of the Advaita school of thought such as orders of reality the identity of the individual soul (atman) and Brahman the concept of Maya the inapplicability of causation to the ultimate reality and Jnana as the direct means to Moksha are all set forth in the Mandukya Karika.

However, the negative tendency is more prominent in his view, since it is in close resemblance with a kind of sunyadava (Nihilism). Although it is not as balanced as Sri Sankaracharya's view, its importance as an attempt to combine in one whole the negative logic of Madhyamika Buddhism with the positive idealism of the Upanishadic thought can not be ignored. Sri Gaudapada Acharya is liable to the change of subjectivism in the traditional sense since he uses the arguments, which the Buddhist Vijnanavadins employed to prove the unreality of the external objects of perception.

The Mandukya Karika explains the doctrine of Maya as the inexplicability of the relation between Atman and the world, the nature or power of Isvara and the apparent dream like appearance of the world. Of these three the first one has been later taken by Sri Sankaracharya and given great prominence in order to develop the school of Advaita into its present form.

The term ‘Advaita’ simply means ‘non-dual’ or ‘not two’. In other words, plainly speaking, the absolute self, the Brahman and the individual self, Jiva are not two. By using the term 'Advaita', it can be said that the scholars prefer to indirectly imply the Unity of the Brahman and the Jiva, rather than stating it directly[16]. Therefore, Advaitins do not directly say that the Jiva and Brahman are one and the same, but say that both are not different from each other.

Chapter 2

The Nature of Bondage

In Advaita we have the concept of ultimate reality, Brahman, developed by Badarayana and Adi Sankara. They took up the idea from the Upanishads where it is denoted by the names, Brahman, Atman, Purusa, Isvara and so forth.

When we consider the world of finite objects from the logical or the cosmological or even the moral point of view, we find that all things and all arguments lead to a supposition of something that is necessarily larger than the finite. Every explanation, every affirmation and denial pertaining to a finite thing involve a reference to something real and more than finite.

In the world, there are many samanyas or universals and all these samanyas in their graduated series are included and comprehended in one great samanya ie; the Brahman, in the nature of a mass of intelligence.

When we say that Brahman is reality, we mean that it is not spatial or temporal. It is not phenomenal or sensible. Brahman is not a thing because it has no attributes. Brahman is not a thing because it has no relations, either spatial or temporal. Brahman has nothing similar to it because it is not a species under a genus. It has no genus. It is the highest universal.

The Brahman is one without a second and is non-dual (Advaita). All descriptions of whole and parts, absolute and relative, finite and infinite are transcendent in Brahman. These descriptions pre- suppose oppositions and opposition characterizes experience.

When we call Brahman as the infinite, we should not equate it as the mere opposite of the finite. To understand the nature of Brahman, we should let go the finite and formal. When the upanisads speak of the Absolute as nirguna (without qualities), what is meant is that it is beyond experience, and beyond the empirical. No gunas, therefore, can belong to the Brahman.

The Brahman is of the nature of ultimate consciousness and yet knows nothing. It is because Brahman is not the consciousness that belongs to a subject that characterizes empirical knowledge. Jnana or knowledge is not its property, but its very essence. Brahman is Jnana. It does not lead to any truth, but it is itself the highest truth.

Brahman is sat because it is not asat. Brahman is cit because it is not acit. Brahman is ananda because it is not of the nature of pain. It is highest truth, perfect being and fullest freedom. The characteristics sat-cit-ananda are not qualities but only negations of non-being. Any quality is a determination and any determination is a negation.

The system of Advaita admits three levels of realties: Prathibhasika satya, vyavaharika satya and Paramarthika satya. Prathibhasika satya is the reality one experience in his state of dreaming It remains true till he wakes up. Vyavaharika satya refers to the empirical reality. It is experienced by many, and hence accepted as true. It lasts till the dawn of Brahma jnana. Paramarthika Satya is the absolute reality or state of Brahman. It is the highest end of all.

Since the mankind views things from the empirical point of view, it demands things to be described in its own way. Thus in the vyavaharika level of reality Brahman is viewed as Saguna against its Nirguna aspect in the Paramarthika level. Thus empirically Brahman is described as Saguna and as the personal god, the creator, the preserver and the refuge of all worlds. Here it is called Isvara. Isvara, in fact is only our conception of Brahman since we are with in the limits of the vyavaharika world. In short, Brahman of Nirguna nature as viewed in the Paramarthika level is the supreme reality.

In Advaita the individual soul is designated as Jiva. According to the Advaitin the Jiva is not a devotee nor a dependent nor a friend nor an equal to the Brahman. It is Brahman it self. Thus Advaita reaches the climax of theistic speculation where, in a sense the soul and the supreme spirit or the self and God is one and the same.

In Advaita, Jiva is nothing else but Brahman itself .Adi Sankaracharya says the difference observed in the empirical level is an illusion and the world itself is a midhya (appearance).

What makes the Jiva think itself to be different from the Brahman is the Bondage in which it finds itself. Thus it takes itself as a body as existing in a Jagat (world) as mortal, as always finite and limited. This happens because, being attached with body it loses the sight of the Paramarthika satya and is confined to the empirical world of name and form (namarupa). Thus, it is only a change in the point of view that causes all the problems for the Jiva. Jiva loses the Paramarthika point of view and in its place take up the less real vyavaharika point of view. It has to remain in this state of imprisonment, where it is limited by avidya or ignorance. It has only finite knowledge and limited powers. It is conditional, pragmatic and psychological. The Jiva is personal due to the presence of the mind (manas), intellect (buddhi) and ego (ahankara).

Jiva is the doer (karmin) and enjoyer (bhoktr). It has the characteristics of merit and demerit, pleasure and pain, attachment and aversion, desire and volition. The Jiva remains in the waking, sleeping and dreaming stages. It is subjected to action, bondage, liberation and transformation. To Jiva, all these state of affairs continue, till the final release, the Moksa, where it is identified with the Brahman.

Karma is one of the bonds that binds the Jiva, and it owns a very important position in the philosophy of Advaita.

The term Karma has two meanings. One is the deed or the action and the other is the fruit of an action. Being attached with the material body the Jiva cannot help doing karmas. It is always doing Karmas. Karmas have their fruits. The doer has to enjoy them irrespective of being good or bad. And this enjoyment leads in to doing further Karmas. They also have their after effects. And this chain continues ad infinitum. In this way the Jiva falls deeper and deeper into the tight grip of Karma. "Mysterious is the way of Karma", says Bhagavad Gita. Where ever the Karma is leading the Jiva or whatever problems it is causing to the Jiva are always unknown and beyond predictions. It leads Jiva from one birth to another and from one Karma to another. Thus it goes on accumulating in the Jiva's account. The classification of Karmas into Prarabdha, Sanchita and agamika is applicable to Advaita also. For not even a single moment, the Jiva is free from karma.

The Advaita suggests Jnana or knowledge as the means to release from the Karma.

No other single term, in the entire history of philosophical world, has triggered off such a vast population of arguments, disputes and controversies as the term Maya has provoked. It is the very basis of the Advaita theory of causation called viverthavada.

The term Maya is derived from the sanskrit root ma which has been used in different senses viz; to measure, to build, to know etc. Generally it means the first one to measure. Thus the Maya means illusive projection of the world by which the immeasurable Brahman appears as if measured.

The problem of one and the many is a vital question to be answered by a monist. He has to explain, how the one becomes many. Hence the doctrine of Maya is cardinal to the school of Advaita Vedanta. Maya is the seed of the world of difference. It is the indescribable world of experience in entirety. Maya is the Principle, which makes the one appear as the many.

Maya is not an entity, not a substance and it does not affect the Brahman. This disparity between appearance and reality is mainly due to the inherent limitation of the Jiva. Maya is the statement of this fact. In Advaita it acts as the connecting link between the infinite and the finite.

The system of Advaita denies any kind of change in the absolute, Brahman. It does not under go any transition. The physical world of multiplicity or Jagat is only a vivertha or appearance. This appearance is due to Maya.

In Vivertha Vada of causation the cause is not transformed into the effect but the true nature of the cause is hidden; screened and in its place the world of variety and form is projected. In Advaita, vivertha stands for the appearance of one, pure, quality less Brahman as characterized by a world of various qualities and attributes.

Brahman, which is beyond the scope of space and time, is brought under the categories of space and time. This is happening due to adhyasa (super imposition). It is exactly as perceiving a snake that is actually not presented. World is Maya. It is only a vyavaharika satya. In order to understand Maya one has to rise from vyavaharika level to the Paramarthika level.

Maya is not real because it can be overcome by Brahma Jnana. Maya is not unreal also, because unlike the "hare's horn" it is not a mere absurdity. It is our subjective mode of experience. Hence Maya is said to be anirvachaniya (that cannot be defined). It is not a substance with a function. It has two properties- avarana (covering) and Vikshepa (projection). Avarana is negative and viksepa is positive. It is through Maya, name and form (bhavarupa) evolve.

As energy of 'Isvara'(Brahman as viewed from empirical level) Maya represents force, power and energy (Sakti). Sakti is the character of Prakriti (primal matter). Maya is therefore, identified with prakrithi. Maya is unintelligent and therefore it is called Jada. Maya is also Anadi (beginning-less).

Maya is inexplicable; in the sense that it is not self - explanatory. For one who knows Brahman there is no Maya. But one who takes his standpoint of logic and reasoning can never understand the relation between Maya and Brahman. It is because to know Brahman is to be Brahman. Thus, through reason, we can never understand how the ultimate is related to the world.

Chapter 3

The concept of Liberation

Advaita is unique in its treatment of knowledge, because it believes that to escape sansara is to know Brahman and to know Brahman is to be Brahman. The point Advaita wants to make clear is that bondage is due to the soul's ignorance. This ignorance is not due to any other reality either inherent or external. The ignorance is like a rope-snake. It ceases to be a snake when knowledge arises. Like wise, with the rise of knowledge of Brahman (Brahma Jnana), all illusions disappear. There occurs Brahmatmaikatva or the realization of the identity of the Atman or self with the Brahman. This is the final end of the life, according to Advaita.

Means to Liberation

As mentioned earlier, Jnana and Jnana alone is the means to attain mukti. Jnana destroys Karma and removes Maya as fire destroys fuel and light removes darkness respectively.

Brahma jnana is a result of study of Vedanta, which includes the learning of the Vedas and the Upanisads. The Vedas and Upanisads are said to be apaurusheya (not created by human beings or God). Since Sruti is the only record of what occurred in moments of exalted imagination, to the minds of saints and sages, there can be nothing that is accidental or contingent in it. They are eternal truths.

The truths that are enshrined in Sruti can be verified by anyone. They are not the exclusive monopoly of the enlightened Ones. But to get the knowledge, one has to go through the disciplines that are laid down for him by the sages.

Sankaracharya speaks of a four fold eligibility (Sadhana chatushtaya) in Vivekachudamani. It consists of Nityanitya vastuviveka, Ihamutra phala bhogaviraga, Samadamadi Sadhana Sampath and Mumukshutva.

Nityanitya Vastuviveka is the ability to discriminate between the transcient (ever changing) and the eternal. The world of senses consists of objects which are transcient. Those which are coming and going cannot be eternal. But there must be some eternal being which is the ground of these eternal things. To know that the self alone is eternal and all else is non-eternal is called Nityanitya vastu viveka.

Ihamutrabhalabhoga viraga is the absence of desire for securing pleasure or avoiding pain here or else where. One should not desire for any kind of this worldly or other worldly pleasures.

Samadamadi sadhana sampath involves attainment of six sadhanas. They are Sama (calmness), Dama (temperance), Titiksha (the spirit of renunciation), Uparathi (fortitude), Sraddha (power of concentration of the mind) and Samadhana (faith in truth).

An aspirant who has attained these six qualities will find that the sacrificial injunctions have no value.

Once the individual attains the three qualities of Nityanitya vastu viveka and Samadamadi Sadhana sampath, he will be a true sanyasin and will have constant desire for freedom.

Mumukshuthva is the earnest desire to know the truth as such. One who attains this eligibility can approach a proper teacher (Guru), who himself is an enlightened one, a released soul (Brahmanishta); to study the Sruti.

Of the four fold path of the Sadhana chatushtaya, it can be seen that earlier one is the cause of the each subsequent one; as, when there is the discrimination between eternal, and non-eternal, there is non-attachment to all kinds of pleasures too; when this detachment is cultivated, there arise samadamadi Sadhana Sampath and so on.

One who performs the four Sadhanas and seeks the help of a proper Guru, can hear from the Guru, the secret of the Upanisads. This stage is called Sravana (hearing). What is heard from the teacher is to be reflected upon to get intellectual conviction.

The disciple is not asked to accept dogmatically whatever is taught by the Guru, even though, the Guru is a competent authority. He can verify it by reasoning (yukti). This stage is called Manana.

But to get direct experience of reality, reason cannot help. Only experience (anubhava) can help. Thus manana is to be followed by the next stage, Dhyana or Niddhidhyasana. Here what has been convinced through reason is to be meditated upon and the result is to be one with that or more correctly, to get Sakshatkara which Sri Sankara designates to be the supreme anubhava, namely, the Advaitanubhuti.

Thus, the procedure is not at all dogmatic. Importance is given to the reason and the experience. Sankaracharya employs the method of objection (purva paksha) and answer (Siddhanta). This is a clear evidence for the Advaitin's disregard for dogmatism.

The Advatins, even when they study the Sruti, are not taking a dogmatic or authoritarian attitude. Even the Sruti is put to the test of reason. They apply Sadlinga or six characteristic marks to examine the Sruti. They are,

a) Upakarma-Upasamhara- The harmony of the initial and concluding passages.

b) Abhyasa- Repetition (purportful passage will repeated).

c) Apurvata- Novelty of the idea.

d) Phala- Fruitfulness.

e) Arthavada- Glorification by enlogistic passages.

f) Upapathi - Intelligibility in the light of reasoning.

Thus, by doing four Sadhanas, listening to the words of the Guru and by the study of Sruthi, one can attain Liberation.

From Advaitin's point of view, Jnana alone liberates. But this assertion does not mean that virtue is of less importance in Advaita. Though non duality is the highest truth, Advaita recognizes a lower stand point where all differences are real. At this level, there is full scope for all the obligations of moral life.

Therefore, the Advaitin accepts all the standards of moral values, as long as he is in the vyavaharika world. They exhort us to avoid sins forbidden by the Sastras. The person, who properly discharges all the obligations, will exhibit certain characteristics, which will qualify him for the study of Vedanta.

According to Sankaracharya, Karma is not the direct means to liberation. Instead, it is the direct means to knowledge. So, one should not give up karmas while he is in the vyavaharika level.

Advaitins accept devotion or Bhakti as essential for the 'vikshepa dosha' of the mind which causes lack of concentration.

Bhakti implies disinterested services to God. So it is also a form of karma. The object of devotion is personal God; Isvara. Isvara is the protector of his devotees. For his grace absolute faith and dependence are necessary.

By devotion, the mind becomes steady. By removed of the vikshepa, one becomes free from the evil desires that make the mind impure. In the absence of vikshepa, one can detach from the various attachments of the world.

When one surrenders himself wholeheartedly to God, he becomes free from all types of the worldly attachments. Thus he can perform his karmas correctly.

However, Bhakti is essential only for whose intellect is fickle. Whose mind is pure and intellect is steady need not take up Bhakti, even though it is not prohibited to him.

Advaita rejects the total synthesis of action, devotion and knowledge. But Advaitins are not against their partial synthesis. It is called Karma Samuchaya.

Karma and Jnana cannot be placed on the same footing. The cessation of the false world of multiplicity and the realization of one's true nature which constitutes liberation is possible only through Jnana; and not through Karma, or Bhakti or Karma and Jnana together or Bhakti-Jnana coordination. Knowledge is the sole means. Therefore, sama samuchaya (total synthesis) of Jnana, Karma and Bhakti is rejected since they are meant for three different levels of intellect.

Mukti

Mukti is the realization of one's own true nature. The Jiva or the soul is always free in its nature and its essence. It is ever infinite, ever conscious and ever blissful. It has the nature of Brahman. It has Brahman.

Owing to ignorance, Jiva does not realize its own essence. So in Advaita, mukti is the process by which the ignorance of the soul is removed, so that the soul can have a clear vision of itself as Brahman. It is the effect of the ignorance that veils the real conscious of the Jiva. Thus, it thinks itself to be different and separate from Brahman. Therefore, according to Advaita Vedanta, mukti is not a new state to be newly attained; but it is the very nature of the self or Jiva.

It is knowledge that can destroy ignorance and bring about mukti. This brings about the self-realization. It is the highest goal of one's life. This realization that results in the identification of the self with Brahman is called Brahmanubhava.

Brahmanubhava is anirvachaniya since it means knowing by being and not a knowing in the ordinary sense of the term. Brahmanubhava gives the highest insight into the Brahman and he who has it knows the answers to every question of the nature of the Brahman as pure being, pure consciousness and pure bliss.

Liberation, in a negative sense, is characterized by the cessation of sorrow, which is an effect of ignorance. Sorrow is the result of the superimposition of the non-self on the self. The self attaches itself to the psycho-physical organism. As a result of liberation, the self realizes that its previous attachment with worldly matters was unreal. This removes misery owing to ignorance. The soul was thinking that it was a worldly creature. But through the knowledge generated by the Vedantic text "Tat tvam asi" (that thou art) the self removes its wrong thought and realizes its true nature.

Again, positively, liberation means the attainment of perfect bliss. Once liberated, the Jiva attains unparalleled happiness. This happiness or infinite bliss is not extrinsic. It is a result of the newly attained power of the discrimination of the eternal from the non-eternal. It is of the nature of Brahman and hence, is the supreme bliss. Here, the happiness and the one who experiences the happiness know no distinctions because the knower of happiness becomes one with the happiness. That is the knower of Brahman becomes one with the Brahman.

To realize the happiness of Brahma Jnana one does not need any ideal, or any effort, since it is eternally established. What is required is the cessation of ignorance and when that is done, the self-luminous Brahman shines of its own accord.

One can achieve mukti while he is alive. This stage of release-while-living is called Jivan mukti. The soul in such a state of release is called Jivan mukta. A Jivan mukta acts as if not living in this world, but he lives in it. He is beyond the world. He does Karmas, but the Karmas are no longer attached to him since he is a released one. The purpose of his Karma is the welfare of the world or loka samgraha.

Jivan Mukta transcends the barriers produced by logic, morality and religion. He guides the world through his acts, speech and thought. He is the spokesman of the Absolute. He is the witness of all things and thoughts, but without the least interest in or attachment with them. He has no desire since he owns the most desired position of release. Though he appears to be living in the world, he is completely beyond its scope and limits.

Though knowledge of absolute reality (BrahmaJnana) removes avidya, the Jivan Mukta's prarabdha Karmas remain. Because of this prarabdha Karma, he has to remain in this world, for the time being. He lives till he finishes off his prarabdha Karma and then leaves his body. This kind of release is called Videhamukti; because, it is the release without the body.

Unlike the Jivan Mukta, the Videhamukta cannot help society. Only the Jivan Mukta can do service for the sake of the society.

Hence, Advaita gives very much importance to the state of Jivan mukti. The Jivan Mukta, being himself liberated, can help others to attain liberation. In the world, he appears as an embodiment of true life, true love and true light. He is a fountain-head of Brahmanubhuti who can lead the aspirants towards Brahman.

Advaita can be regarded as the climax of philosophy, pinnacle of thought that dares to equate the Individual Self with the Supreme Absolute Self, beyond which no thinker can ever pass.

www.ingramcontent.com/pod-product-compliance
Ingram Content Group UK Ltd.
Pitfield, Milton Keynes, MK11 3LW, UK
UKHW041836200726
13854UKWH00003BA/1167